EXPLORING THE STATES

Ohio

THE BUCKEYE STATE

by Amy Rechner

BELLWETHER MEDIA · MINNEAPOLIS, MN

Note to Librarians, Teachers, and Parents:

Blastoff! Readers are carefully developed by literacy experts and combine standards-based content with developmentally appropriate text.

Level 1 provides the most support through repetition of high-frequency words, light text, predictable sentence patterns, and strong visual support.

Level 2 offers early readers a bit more challenge through varied simple sentences, increased text load, and less repetition of high-frequency words.

Level 3 advances early-fluent readers toward fluency through increased text and concept load, less reliance on visuals, longer sentences, and more literary language.

Level 4 builds reading stamina by providing more text per page, increased use of punctuation, greater variation in sentence patterns, and increasingly challenging vocabulary.

Level 5 encourages children to move from "learning to read" to "reading to learn" by providing even more text, varied writing styles, and less familiar topics.

Whichever book is right for your reader, Blastoff! Readers are the perfect books to build confidence and encourage a love of reading that will last a lifetime!

This edition first published in 2014 by Bellwether Media, Inc.

No part of this publication may be reproduced in whole or in part without written permission of the publisher. For information regarding permission, write to Bellwether Media, Inc., Attention: Permissions Department, 5357 Penn Avenue South, Minneapolis, MN 55419.

Library of Congress Cataloging-in-Publication Data

Rechner, Amy.
 Ohio / by Amy Rechner.
  pages cm. – (Blastoff! readers. Exploring the states)
 Includes bibliographical references and index.
 Summary: "Developed by literacy experts for students in grades three through seven, this book introduces young readers to the geography and culture of Ohio"–Provided by publisher.
 ISBN 978-1-62617-034-6 (hardcover : alk. paper)
 1. Ohio–Juvenile literature. I. Title.
 F491.3.R39 2014
 977.1–dc23

2013005694

Printed in the United States of America, North Mankato, MN.

Table of Contents

Where Is Ohio?

Ohio lies in the **Midwest** region of the United States. Lake Erie, one of the **Great Lakes**, stretches along its northern border. To the northwest is the state of Michigan. Indiana is Ohio's western neighbor. West Virginia and Pennsylvania share the eastern border. Kentucky lies to the south.

Ohio's capital, Columbus, sits in the center of the state. Many of Ohio's larger cities are near bodies of water. Toledo and Cleveland are on Lake Erie in the north. In the southwest, Cincinnati stands on the banks of the mighty Ohio River.

Indiana

Did you know?
Columbus was named the state capital in 1812. However, the city did not yet exist. It was built after the location was chosen.

Canada

Michigan

Lake Erie

Toledo

Cleveland

Pennsylvania

Ohio

Columbus ★

Ohio River

Hocking Hills ●

West Virginia

Cincinnati

N

W ✦ E

S

Kentucky

5

For thousands of years, **Native** Americans hunted and lived in what is now Ohio. The first Europeans arrived around 1670. Fur traders from France and England soon followed. In 1763, Britain took over the Ohio Territory. After the **Revolutionary War**, the new United States gained control. Ohio became a state in 1803.

fur trade

Ohio Timeline!

1670:	French explorer René-Robert Cavelier travels from Canada to Ohio. He claims the land for France.
1763:	Great Britain wins control of Ohio from France.
1783:	The Ohio Territory becomes part of the new United States.
1795:	After years of battle, Native Americans surrender about two-thirds of present-day Ohio to the United States.
1803:	Ohio becomes the seventeenth state.
1832:	The Ohio and Erie Canal is completed. It links Lake Erie with the Ohio River.
1852:	Ohio author Harriet Beecher Stowe publishes *Uncle Tom's Cabin*. The book shows the evils of slavery.
1903:	Orville and Wilbur Wright fly their plane for the first time. They built it in their Dayton bicycle shop.
1969:	Ohio native Neil Armstrong is the first person to walk on the moon.

Harriet Beecher Stowe

Neil Armstrong

Wright brothers

The Land

Long ago, **glaciers** crept across much of Ohio's land. They left behind rolling **plains** of rich soil. Southeast Ohio has steep hills and deep valleys. Thick forests cover this region. In eastern Ohio, giant salt deposits lie underground. They formed when an ancient sea dried up around 400 million years ago.

In addition to Lake Erie and the Ohio River, Ohio has many important waterways. The Sandusky, Great Miami, and Scioto are major rivers. Ohio has cold winters and hot, sticky summers. Cities along Lake Erie often get deep snowfall. Heavy rains sometimes cause flooding.

fun fact

Kelleys Island in Lake Erie has rare glacial grooves on its north side. A glacier carved these long grooves into the bedrock about 18,000 years ago.

Kelleys Island

Ohio's Climate

average °F

spring
Low: 39°
High: 60°

summer
Low: 61°
High: 81°

fall
Low: 44°
High: 62°

winter
Low: 21°
High: 37°

Hocking Hills

The Hocking Hills region is filled with amazing rock formations. Over millions of years, wind and water wore down the sandstone bedrock in southern Ohio. These natural forces carved out towering cliffs, rock arches, and **recess caves**.

Old Man's Cave

Did you know?
Old Man's Cave got its name after a man lived in the cave in the late 1700s!

The Rock House

! **fun fact**
The Rock House is a famous cave in Hocking Hills State Park. The long, rocky tunnel sits halfway up the side of a cliff. It has spaces that look like windows along its side.

Old Man's Cave is a big recess cave next to a deep **gorge**. Waterfalls pour into the creek at the gorge's bottom. Below the cave is a pool of churning water called the Devil's Bathtub. Hiking trails take visitors to Old Man's Cave and throughout Hocking Hills State Park.

Wildlife

Large animals such as black bears are rarely seen in Ohio. However, white-tailed deer roam throughout the state. Beavers, muskrats, and foxes live in woodlands and near water. Perch and trout swim in Ohio's rivers. Snapping turtles like to hide in lakes and streams with muddy bottoms. Seabirds such as gulls and terns swoop over Lake Erie.

Most of Ohio's forests have been cleared, but woodlands remain in the southeast. Blue jays and cardinals fly among the trees of **hardwood forests**. Purple coneflowers, violets, and other wildflowers bloom across the state.

tern

snapping turtle

muskrat

cardinal

13

Landmarks

National Museum
of the U.S. Air Force

Did you know?

Ohio had the most active Underground Railroad network of any state. About 3,000 miles (4,828 kilometers) of routes took runaway slaves from the Ohio River to safe places in the north.

History fans have plenty to see in Ohio. They can tour old houses that served as stopping points along the **Underground Railroad**. Nearby museums tell more about Ohio's efforts to fight **slavery**. Near Dayton, the National Museum of the U.S. Air Force displays early planes and missiles. A special part of the museum shows a spacecraft from the Apollo moon missions.

Serpent Mound is an ancient **earthwork** in southern Ohio. Native peoples known as Mound Builders created it more than 900 years ago. The waist-high structure is more than 1,300 feet (396 meters) long. From above, it looks like a giant slithering snake.

Serpent Mound

Underground Railroad exhibit

Cleveland

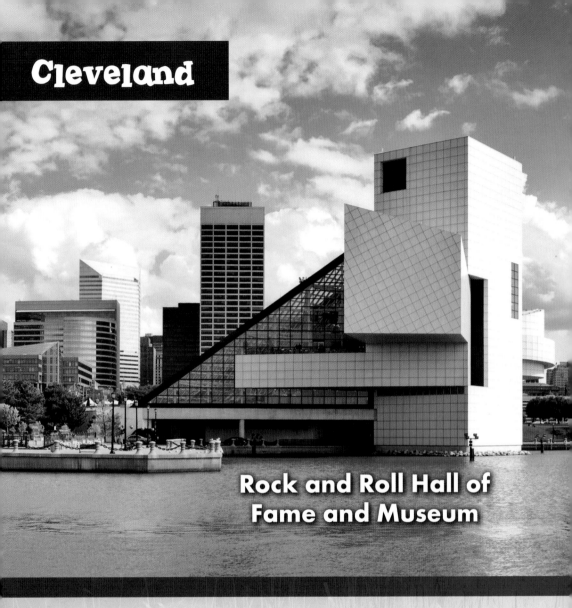

Rock and Roll Hall of Fame and Museum

Cleveland's steel factories and shipping activity brought people from many different countries to the city on Lake Erie. Today, the Little Italy neighborhood is home to Italian markets and restaurants. Slavic Village was once home to **immigrants** from Eastern Europe. Many people still speak Polish there.

Cleveland Zoo

Edgewater State Park

Cleveland has a zoo and many museums. The most famous museum is the Rock and Roll Hall of Fame and Museum. Visitors can see **artifacts** from famous musicians including the Beatles, Madonna, and U2. Edgewater State Park in downtown Cleveland has beautiful sand beaches along the Lake Erie shore.

Working

Swiss cheese
making

18

In Ohio's early days, its rich land attracted miners and farmers. Coal, natural gas, and salt are still mined today. Farmers grow soybeans, corn, and other vegetables. Lake Erie and Ohio's web of rivers make the state an important center for shipping and transportation. Goods pass through the **ports** at Sandusky and Toledo.

Ohio is one of the nation's leading producers of steel. Factories make automobiles, tires, and cleaning products. Most Ohio workers have **service jobs**. They work in hospitals, banks, restaurants, and offices.

Where People Work in Ohio

manufacturing
11%

services
75%

farming and
natural resources
2%

government
12%

Playing

Ohioans take fun seriously. They enjoy hiking, fishing, and biking in the many state parks. Thrill-seekers visit the Cedar Point amusement park near Sandusky or Kings Island near Cincinnati. Lake Erie's beaches draw crowds for picnics and water fun.

Plays and concerts draw people to Cincinnati and Cleveland. Children's theater companies perform in several Ohio cities. Sports fans follow the many professional teams in the state. Everyone cheers for Ohio State University's Buckeyes.

Cedar Point amusement park

Lake Erie

Ohio State Buckeyes football game

Ohio Buckeyes

Ingredients:

1 1/2 cups peanut butter

1/2 cup butter, softened

1 teaspoon vanilla extract

1/8 teaspoon salt

3 3/4 cups powdered sugar

4 cups semisweet chocolate chips

Directions:

1. In a large bowl, mix together all ingredients except chocolate chips. The dough will look dry.

2. Roll into 1-inch balls and place on a waxed paper-lined cookie sheet. Poke a toothpick into the top of each ball. Chill in freezer until firm, about 30 minutes.

3. Melt chocolate chips in microwave until smooth, stirring every 30 seconds.

4. Dip frozen peanut butter balls in chocolate using toothpick as a handle. Leave a spot of peanut butter showing at the top to make them look like buckeyes.

5. Put back on the cookie sheet and refrigerate until serving.

Cincinnati chili

kebabs

Ohio was settled by people from many different countries. They brought their favorite foods with them to the new land. Clevelanders enjoy Italian ice cream and pasta as well as Polish sausages and pastries. Toledo offers **kebabs** and other Middle Eastern foods. **Amish** people serve simple, hearty dishes such as chicken and noodles.

Cincinnati is known for its German food, but it is even more famous for chili. Restaurants called chili parlors attract visitors for this local favorite. Cincinnati chili is served over spaghetti with cheese, onions, and beans on top.

Festivals

Ohio's festivals celebrate the state's unique traits. Hinckley Township observes **Buzzard** Day every March. Flocks of the large birds return to the area to roost each spring. In Canton, the Pro Football Hall of Fame hosts an **Enshrinement** Festival. Fans cheer for the newest members of the Hall of Fame in a special parade.

The Vectren Dayton Air Show takes off in August. Daredevil pilots and military aircraft share the skies for a thrilling show. The Ohio State Fair in Columbus offers music, rides, and livestock shows. The Taste of Cincinnati gives visitors a chance to sample food from the city's many restaurants.

fun fact

Twinsburg hosts the world's largest annual gathering of twins. Twins Days welcomes twins, triplets, and other multiples of all ages.

Ohio State Fair

The Amish

Ohio is home to the world's largest Amish community. Amish people first arrived in the state in the 1800s. In many ways, they still live as though it were that time.

Amish people do not own cars, computers, televisions, or even telephones. They believe that it is wrong to give attention to technology instead of family and neighbors. Many Amish are farmers or furniture makers. They also run hotels, restaurants, and shops for **tourists**. From simple Amish farms to bustling waterfront cities, Ohio brings together the best of the nation's past and present.

! fun fact

Visitors to Amish Country need to drive carefully. They have to share the road with carriages and farm machinery pulled by horses!

Fast Facts About Ohio

Ohio's Flag

The flag of Ohio has a unique shape. It ends in a V-shaped cut called a swallowtail. The flag shows a blue triangle on the left side. Red and white stripes extend from it. In the triangle are 17 stars to mark Ohio's place as the 17th state. A white circle with a red center stands for the "O" in Ohio.

State Flower
scarlet carnation

State Nickname:	The Buckeye State
State Motto:	"With God, All Things Are Possible"
Year of Statehood:	1803
Capital City:	Columbus
Other Major Cities:	Cleveland, Cincinnati
Population:	11,536,504 (2010)
Area:	44,825 square miles (116,096 square kilometers); Ohio is the 34th largest state.
Major Industries:	manufacturing, mining, transportation
Natural Resources:	waterways, farmland, coal, oil, natural gas, limestone, salt
State Government:	99 representatives; 33 senators
Federal Government:	16 representatives; 2 senators
Electoral Votes:	18

State Bird
northern cardinal

State Animal
white-tailed deer

Glossary

Amish—a Christian group that came to North America from Switzerland and Germany in the 1700s

artifacts—objects of historical value

buzzard—a type of large bird that hunts prey

earthwork—a structure built from dirt and rocks, such as a wall or mound

enshrinement—the act of putting something on display to be admired

glaciers—massive sheets of ice that cover large areas of land

gorge—a deep, narrow valley with steep, rocky sides

Great Lakes—five large freshwater lakes on the border between the United States and Canada

hardwood forests—forests made mostly of trees that lose their leaves in fall

immigrants—people who leave one country to live in another country

kebabs—cubes of meat and vegetables cooked on skewers

Midwest—a region of 12 states in the north-central United States

native—originally from a specific place

plains—large areas of flat land

ports—harbors where ships can dock

recess caves—above-ground caves that were carved into the side of rock

Revolutionary War—the war between 1775 and 1783 in which the United States fought for independence from Great Britain

service jobs—jobs that perform tasks for people or businesses

slavery—a system in which certain people are considered property

tourists—people who travel to visit another place

Underground Railroad—a network of secret routes and safe houses that helped slaves in the South escape to freedom in the North

To Learn More

AT THE LIBRARY

Nolen, Jerdine. *Eliza's Freedom Road: An Underground Railroad Diary*. New York, N.Y.: Simon & Schuster Books for Young Readers, 2011.

Stille, Darlene. *Ohio*. New York, N.Y.: Children's Press, 2009.

Weir, William. *The Wright Brothers: The First to Fly*. New York, N.Y.: PowerKids Press, 2013.

ON THE WEB

Learning more about Ohio is as easy as 1, 2, 3.

1. Go to www.factsurfer.com.

2. Enter "Ohio" into the search box.

3. Click the "Surf" button and you will see a list of related Web sites.

With factsurfer.com, finding more information is just a click away.

Index

The images in this book are reproduced through the courtesy of: drnadig, front cover; Timewatch Images/ Alamy, p. 6; (Collection)/ Prints & Photographs Division/ Library of Congress, p. 7 (left, right); Photri Images/ Alamy, p. 7 (middle); Stan Rohrer/ Alamy, p. 8 (small); kathmanduphotog, pp. 8-9; Doug Lemke, pp. 10-11; Kenneth Keifer, p. 11 (top); Doug Lemke, p. 11 (bottom); Byrdyak, p. 12 (top); Melissa Brandes, p. 12 (middle); Sergey Uryadnikov, p. 12 (bottom); gregg williams, pp. 12-13; Chiltern Image Service/ Alamy, p. 14; SuperStock/ GlowImages, p. 15 (left); William Manning/ Alamy, p. 15 (right); drnadig, pp. 16-17; AP Photo/ Mark Duncan, p. 17 (top); Jeff Greenberg/ Alamy, p. 17 (bottom); Nicolas McComber/ Getty Images, p. 18; Ramona Heim, p. 19; Dennis MacDonald/ Alamy, p. 20 (top); Denise Kappa, p. 20 (bottom); Aaron Josefczyk/ Icon SMI/ Newscom, pp. 20-21; Zigzag Mountain Art, p. 22; wsmahar, p. 23 (top); tlorna, p. 23 (bottom); National Geographic Image Collection/ Alamy, p. 24 (small); Stan Rohrer/ Alamy, p. 25; AP Photo/ Tony Dejak, pp. 26-27; Delmas Lehman, p. 27; Pakmor, p. 28 (top); terekhov igor, p. 28 (bottom); Steve Byland, p. 29 (left); Tony Campbell, p. 29 (right).